Canadian Symbols

The Canadian Flag

by Sabrina Crewe

CAPSTONE PRESS
a capstone imprint

Pebble Plus is published by Capstone Press,
1710 Roe Crest Drive, North Mankato, Minnesota 56003
www.capstonepub.com

Library of Congress Cataloging-in-Publication Data
Cataloging-in-publication information is on file with the Library of Congress.

ISBN 978–1-4914-7090-9 (library binding : alk. paper)
ISBN 978–1-4914-7096-1 (pbk. : alk. paper)
ISBN 978–1-4914-7108-1 (eBook PDF)

Developed and Produced by Discovery Books Limited
Paul Humphrey: project manager
Sabrina Crewe: editor
Ian Winton: designer

Photo Credits
SurangaSL/Shutterstock: cover; Meunierd/Shutterstock: title page; Gary718/Shutterstock: 5; Rawpixel/Shutterstock: 7; Duncan Cameron, Library and Archives Canada, PA-168019: 9; Muskoka Stock Photos/Shutterstock: 11; Sianc/Shutterstock: 13; Paolo Bona/Shutterstock: 15; David P. Lewis/Shutterstock: 17; John E. Sokolowski/Hamilton Tiger-Cats Football Club: 19; Andre St. Louis/Shutterstock: 21.

Note to Parents and Teachers
This book describes and illustrates the Canadian flag. The images support early readers in understanding text. The repetition of words and phrases helps early readers learn new words. This book also introduces early readers to subject-specific vocabulary words, which are defined in the Glossary section. Early readers may need assistance to read some words and to use the Table of Contents, Glossary, Read More, Internet Sites, and Index sections of the book.

Printed in China through World Print Ltd in 2014
007272WPS15

Table of Contents

A Symbol for Canada

A symbol is a picture or thing that stands for something important. Symbols can stand for ideas, beliefs, and countries. The Canadian flag is a symbol of Canada.

The Canadian flag always flies on the Peace Tower on Parliament Hill in Ottawa.

Flag History

People have always used flags to claim places. Rulers had flags to show their power. Countries use their national flags in the same way. Their flags are their most important symbols.

Flags from many countries fly together.

Canada's Maple Leaf flag
first flew on February 15,
1965. February 15 is now
Flag Day in Canada.
On Flag Day, Canadians
celebrate their country.

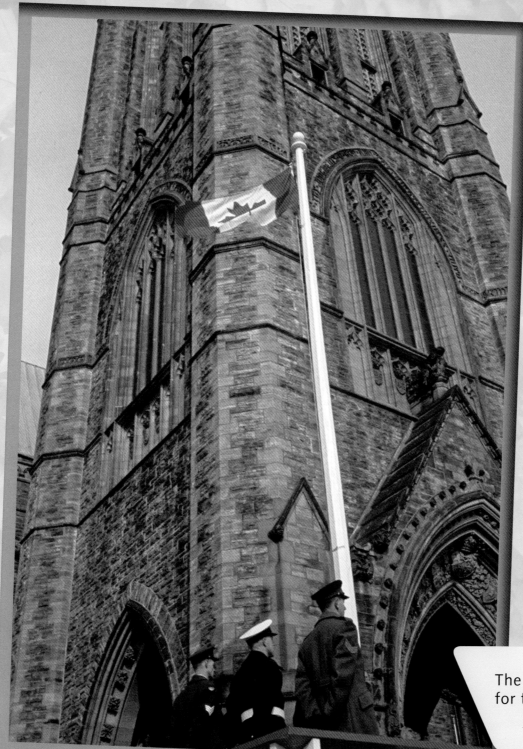

The Maple Leaf flag was raised for the first time in 1965.

Parts of the Flag

The Canadian flag has one large white stripe in the middle and a smaller red stripe on each side. Red and white are Canada's national colours.

The white stripe is twice as wide as the red stripes.

The maple leaf on our flag is from the maple tree. Maple trees have always been important to Canadians. That is why Canada uses the maple leaf as a symbol.

Maple syrup comes from the sap of a maple tree.

13

All over the world, people know the maple leaf stands for Canada. It's easy to recognize our flag because of the maple leaf!

Olympic athletes wear maple leaves to show they are Canadians.

Celebrating with Flags

The Canadian flag is a symbol of unity among Canadian people. We use the flag to celebrate our country. We wave flags to show that we are proud of Canada.

Celebrating with flags on Canada Day

Some flags are too big to fly!
One huge flag is rolled out at
the Hamilton Tiger-Cats football
games. It takes 80 people to
hold it up.

Canada's biggest flag

Canada's regions have their own special flags. Canada's three territories and ten provinces fly their special flags in their areas. Sometimes the thirteen flags all fly together with the national flag.

Canada's fourteen flags

Glossary

national—something that belongs to the whole country

provinces—ten large parts of Canada

region—an area that is part of a country

sap—liquid that carries food and water inside plants, including trees

symbol—something that stands for something else. People use symbols to show what is important to them.

territories—three large parts of Canada

unity—when people or parts of something come together into one whole

Read More

Owens, Ann-Maureen and **Jane Yealland**. *Our Flag: The Story of Canada's Maple Leaf*. Toronto, ON: Kids Can Press, 2014.

Trottier, Maxine. *Our Canadian Flag*. Markham, ON: Scholastic Canada, 2005.

Internet Sites

FactHound offers a safe, fun way to find Internet sites related to this book. All of the sites on FactHound have been researched by our staff.

Here's all you do:

Visit *www.facthound.com*

Type in this code: 9781491470909

Check out projects, games and lots more at
www.capstonekids.com

Index